AF598993

American Sign Language

School

by E. Russell Primm III • illustrated by Kathleen Petelinsek

childsworld.com

Published by The Child's World®
800-599-READ • childsworld.com

Copyright © 2025 by The Child's World®
All rights reserved. No part of this book may be reproduced or utilized in any form or by any means without written permission from the publisher.

Photography Credits
PeopleImages.com–Yuri A/Shutterstock.com, cover, 1, 5, 7; Prostock-studio/Shutterstock.com, 3; Ground Picture/Shutterstock.com, 4; Monkey Business Images/Shutterstock.com, 6, 9; Oksana Kuzmina/Shutterstock.com, 8; Peter Kniez/Shutterstock.com, 10; SeventyFour/Shutterstock.com, 11, 15, 19; Marie C Fields/Shutterstock.com, 12; StanislauV/Shutterstock.com, 13; Donga Bonga/Shutterstock.com, 14; FAMILY STOCK/Shutterstock.com, 16; New Africa/Shutterstock.com, 17; roopankit/Shutterstock.com, 18; PEPPERSMINT/Shutterstock.com, 20; Zyn Chakrapong/Shutterstock.com, 21

ISBN Information
9781503889057 (Reinforced Library Binding)
9781503890138 (Portable Document Format)
9781503891371 (Online Multi-user eBook)
9781503892613 (Electronic Publication)

LCCN 2023950183

Printed in the United States of America

Note to Parents, Caregivers, and Educators: The understanding of any language begins with the acquisition of vocabulary, whether the language is spoken or manual. The books in this series provide readers, both young and old, with basic American Sign Language signs. Combining close photo cues and simple, but detailed, line illustrations, children and adults alike can begin the process of learning American Sign Language.

Let these books be an introduction to the world of American Sign Language. Most languages have regional dialects and multiple ways of expressing the same thought. This is also true for sign language. We have attempted to use the most common version of the signs for the words in this series. As with any language, the best way to learn is to be taught in person by a frequent user. It is our hope that this series will pique your interest in sign language.

A special thanks to our advisers: As a member of a deaf family that spans four generations, **Kim Bianco Majeri** lives, works, and plays among the Deaf community. **Carmine L. Vozzolo** is an educator of children who are deaf and hard of hearing, as well as their families.

E. Russell Primm III was a well-known figure in the publishing industry who produced thousands of acclaimed books for children. He was affiliated with organizations such as the American Library Association, the Chicago Book Clinic, and the University of Chicago Publishing Program Advisory Board.

Kathleen Petelinsek has loved books since she was a child. Through the years, she has written, designed, and illustrated many books for children. She lives in Wisconsin, near her granddaughter who also shares her love for books.

See page 23 to learn how to sign all the letters.

Bus

1\.

2\.

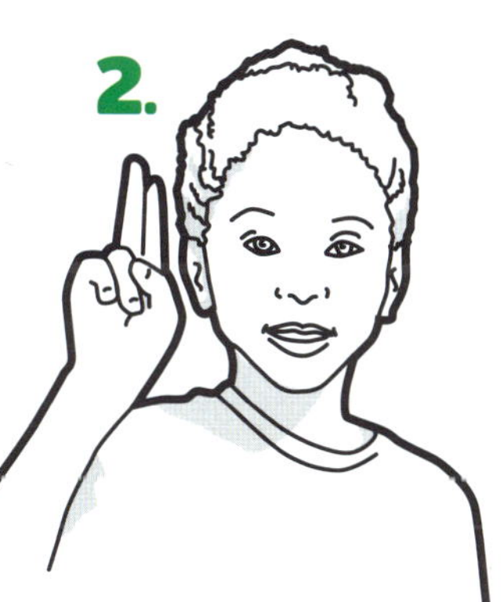

3\.

Spell B-U-S with your fingers.

What is your school mascot?

School

Face your palms together as shown. Clap your hands together twice.

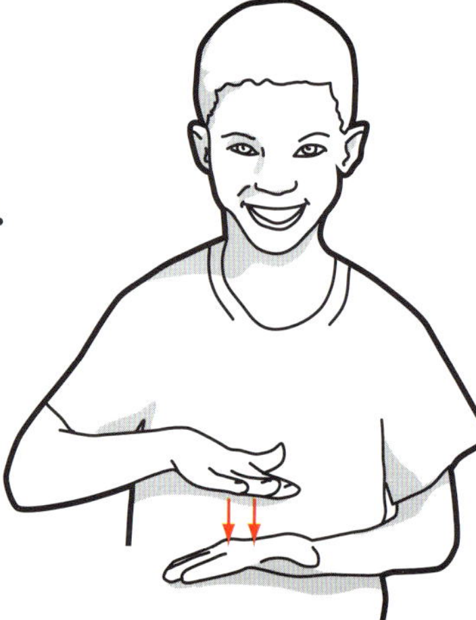

What is your favorite class?

Class

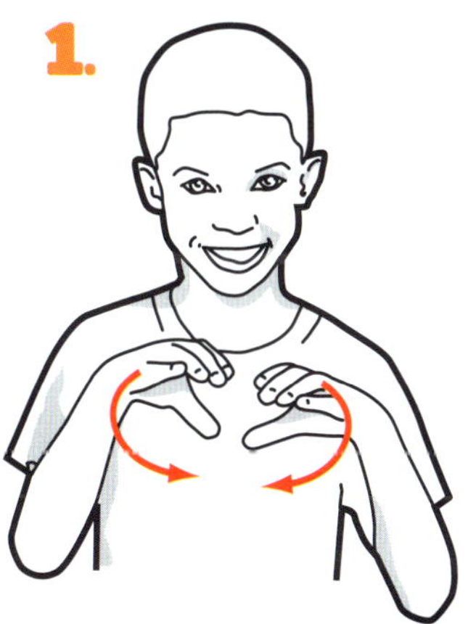

Make the "C" sign with both hands facing each other. Then roll your wrists so that your pinkies touch.

Backpacks are also called "rucksacks" or "knapsacks."

Backpack

Tap your chest with your thumbs.

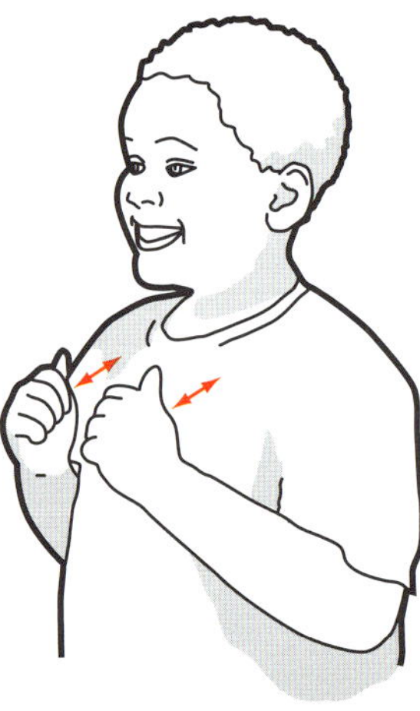

Students began using desks in school in the 1880s.

Desk

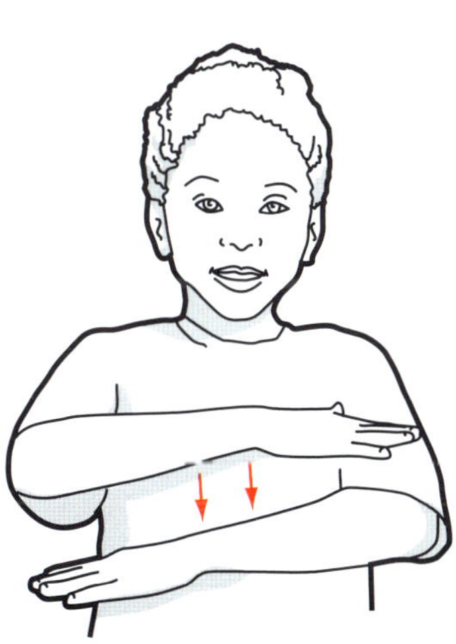

Move your right arm down and tap your left arm twice.

Raising your hand is the right way to ask a question in class.

Student

Close your fingers together as you move your hand toward your forehead. Then face palms together and motion downward.

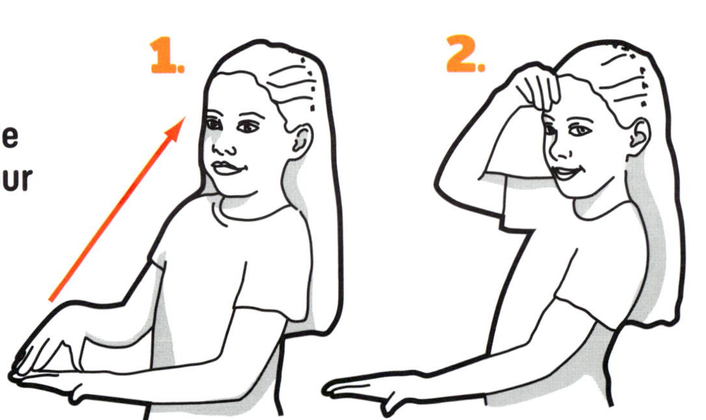

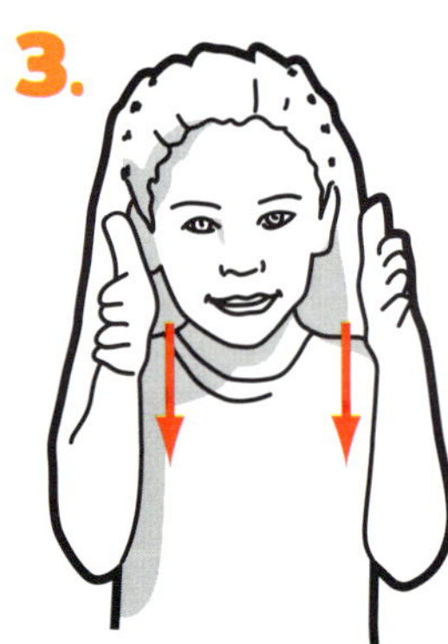

Teachers do a lot of hard work every day.

Teacher

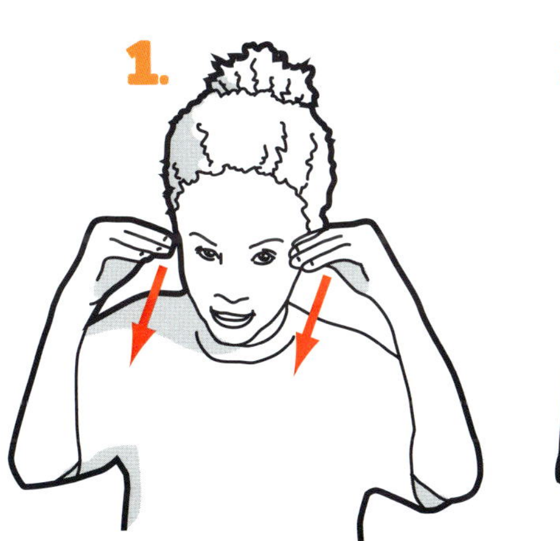

Move your hands outward, away from your forehead. Then face your palms together and move downward.

What is your favorite book?

Book

Open your hands as if you are opening a book.

Do you love books? You could be a librarian when you grow up!

Library

Make the letter "L" and circle clockwise. (The person you are speaking to will see the sign go counterclockwise.)

The idea for wooden pencils started about 500 years ago.

Pencil

Touch your fingers to your mouth. Then pretend to write on your left hand.

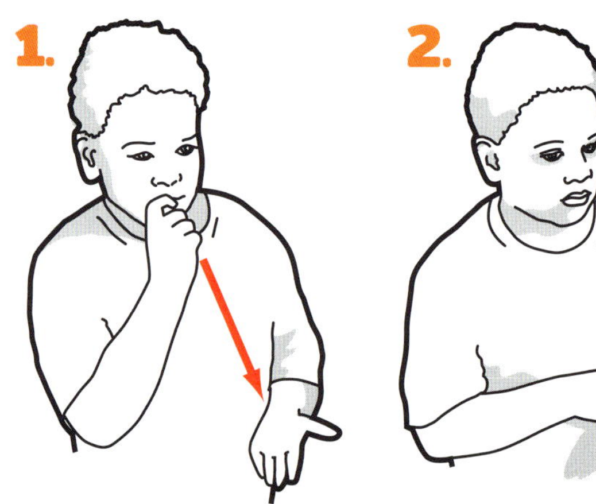

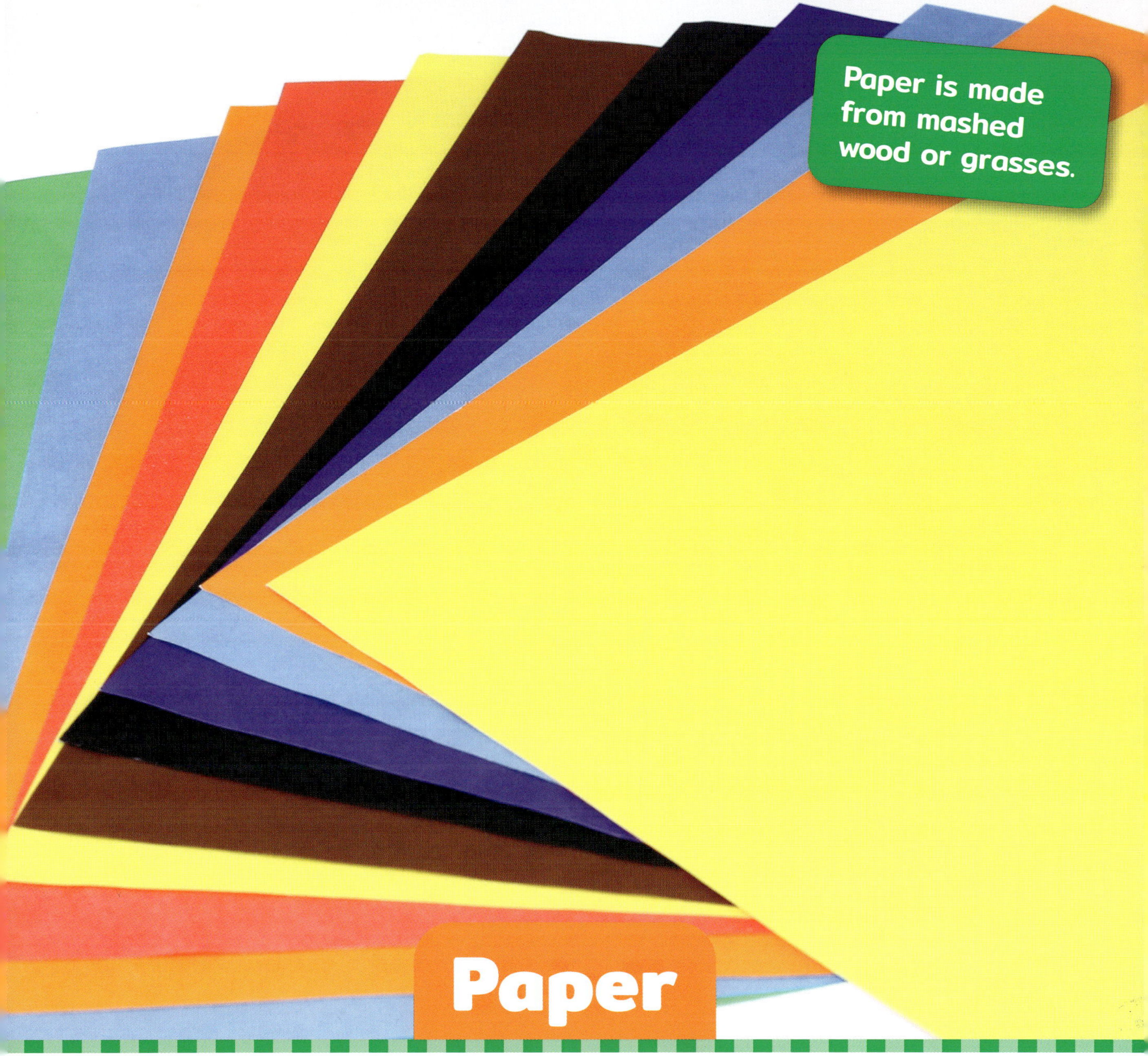

Paper is made from mashed wood or grasses.

Paper

Have both hands flat. Face your palms together and sweep your right hand across your left hand, toward your body. Repeat.

Paint has been around for about 100,000 years!

Paint

Move your right hand up and down against your left hand as if you were using a paintbrush.

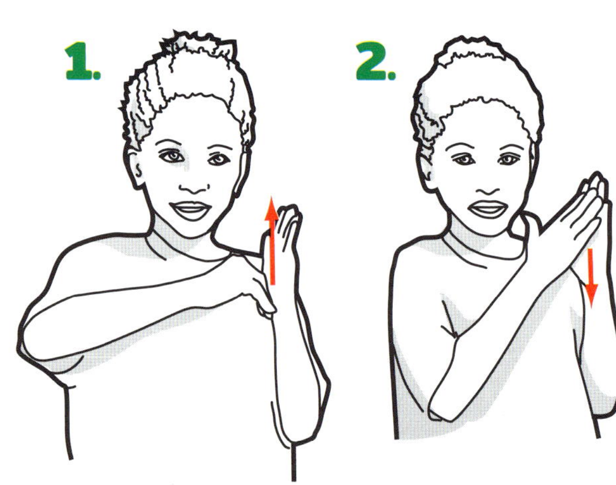

Have you used glue for a project in art class?

Glue

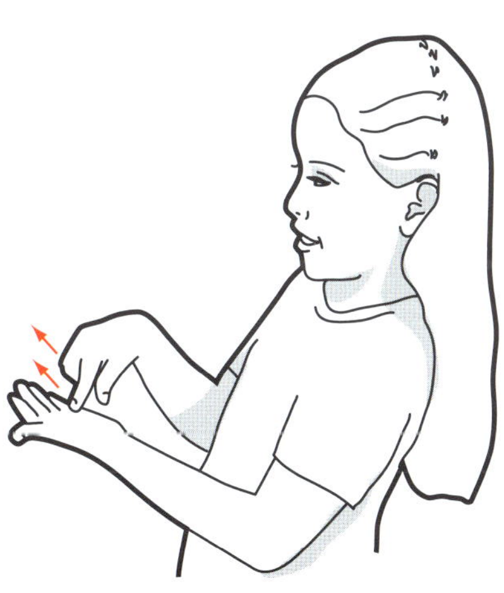

Make the letter "G" with your right hand. Move your fingers along your flat left hand from the palm to the fingers.

Scissors have been around for about 500 years.

Scissors

Move your fingers like scissors.

Erasers are made from rubber.

Eraser

Make a fist. Move it over your flat left hand as if you are erasing something.

Crayons are made of wax. If they get hot enough, they can melt.

Crayons

Wiggle all your fingers a little by your mouth. Then pretend to write on your hand.

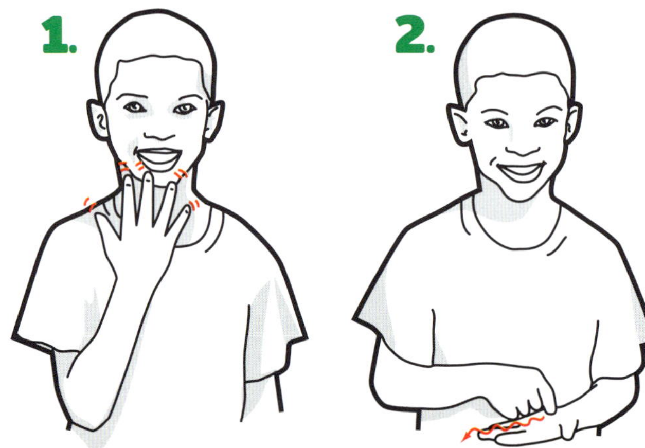

Many computers today are laptops, like this one.

Computer

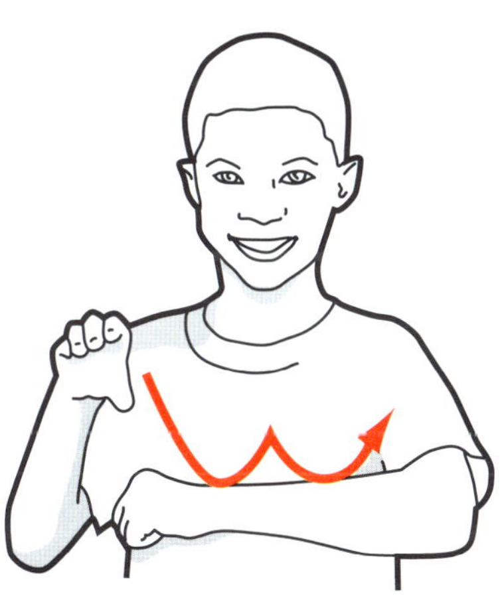

Make the letter "C" with your right hand. Brush your thumb twice on your left arm.

The part of a bell that makes the sound is called the "clapper."

Bell

Your index finger hits your flat hand.

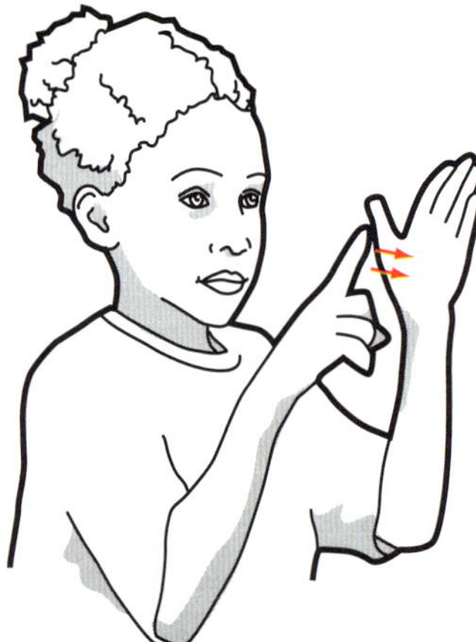

What is your favorite thing to do at a playground?

Playground

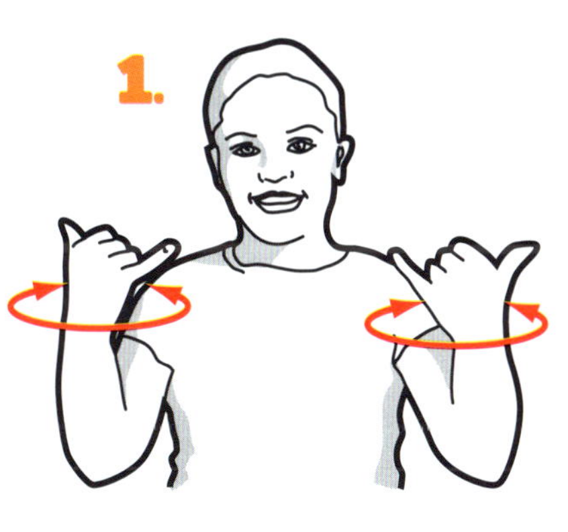

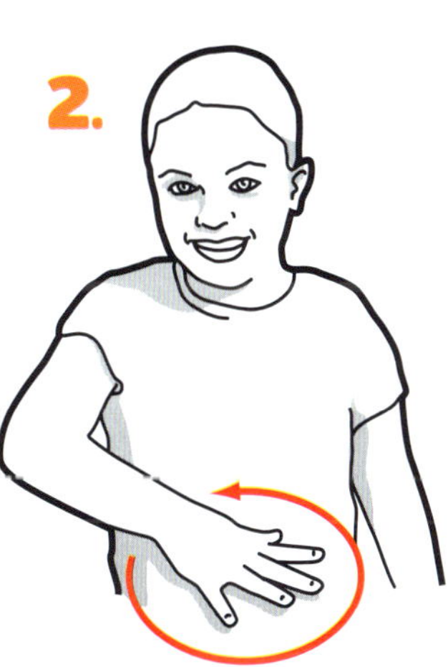

Make the "Y" shape with both hands. Flick them twice. Then with your right hand, make a flat circle.

Wonder More

- How much did you know about American Sign Language (ASL) before reading this book? Do you already know some ASL signs? What new signs did you learn?

- Some words or specific names don't have signs. In these cases, you can spell the individual letters of the word, which is called fingerspelling. Look at the alphabet chart on page 23. Can you sign the letters in your name?

- With a partner, pick three signs from this book and practice them together. Are you able to understand each other? Is ASL easier or harder than you thought it would be?

- Did you know that your facial expression can affect the meaning of a sign? Why do you think our facial expressions are an important part of communication in ASL?

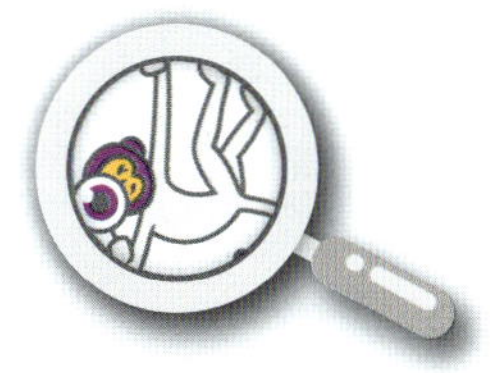

Sign Language Alphabet

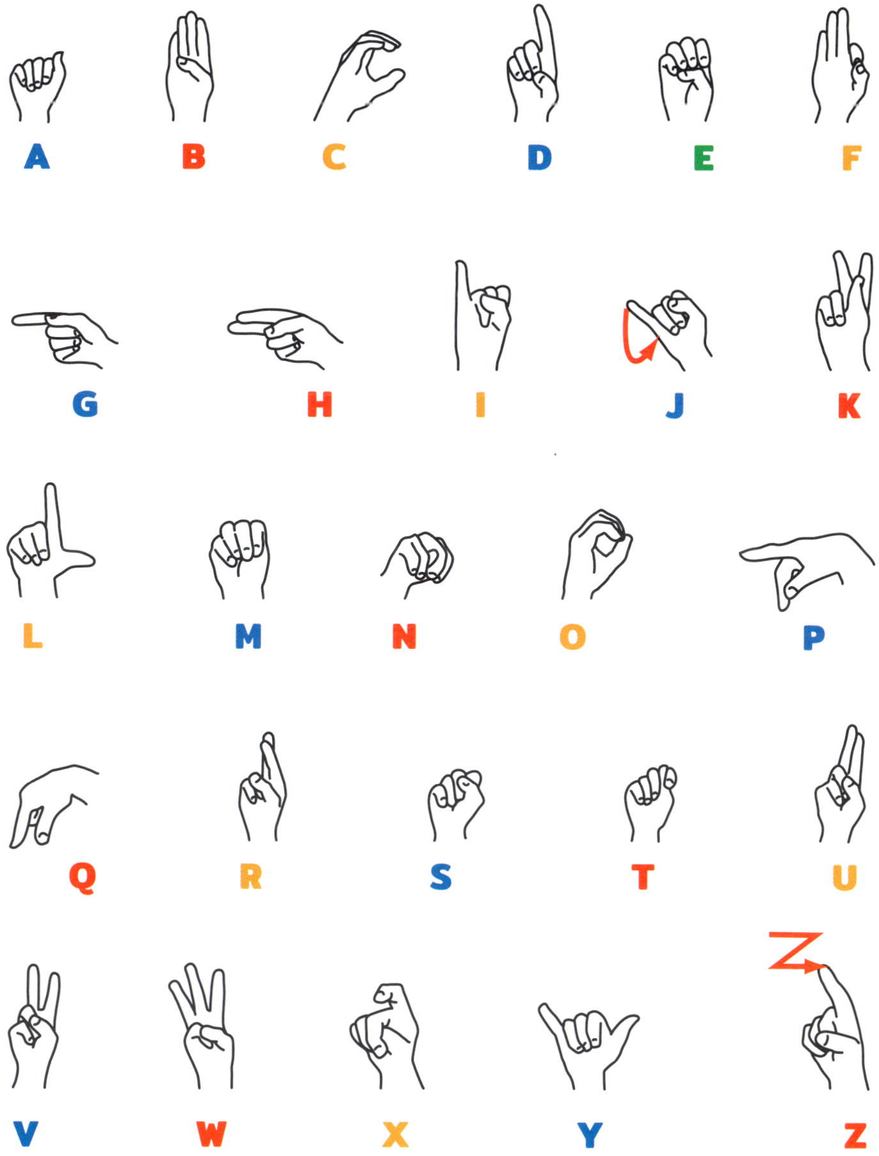

A B C D E F

G H I J K

L M N O P

Q R S T U

V W X Y Z

Find Out More

In the Library

Adams, Tara, and Natalia Sanabria (illustrator). *We Can Sign! An Essential Guide to American Sign Language for Kids*. Emeryville, CA: Rockridge Press, 2020.

Martin, Ann M., and Chan Chau (illustrator). *Jessi's Secret Language: A Graphic Novel* (The Baby-Sitters Club Graphix). New York, NY: Scholastic, 2022.

On the Web

Visit our website for links about American Sign Language:
childsworld.com/links

Note to Parents, Caregivers, Teachers, and Librarians: We routinely verify our web links to make sure they are safe and active sites. So encourage your readers to check them out!

A Special Thank-You!

Thank you to our models from the Program for Children Who are Deaf and Hard of Hearing at the Alexander Graham Bell School in Chicago, Illinois.

Alina's favorite things to do are art, soccer, and swimming. DJ is her brother!

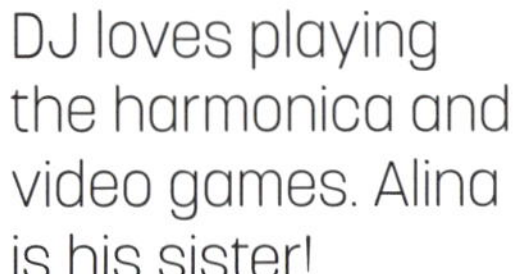

DJ loves playing the harmonica and video games. Alina is his sister!

Dareous likes football. His favorite team is the Detroit Lions. He also likes to play video games.

Jasmine likes writing and math in school. She also loves to swim.

Darionna likes the swings and merry-go-round on the playground. She also loves art.